THEN & NOW

JACKSON COUNTY

Opposite: This image dates to 1895, when Sylva was not yet Jackson's county seat. Looking down from the Jackson Street area, the prominent structure with the peaked roof was located to the right of the C. J. Harris Building, which houses the present-day Jackson's General Store. Early industrialist Harris's signature building would not be constructed until some eight years later. (Courtesy of Lynn Hotaling.)

THEN & NOW

JACKSON COUNTY

Nick Breedlove and Lynn Hotaling

To Herald *publishers Jim and Steve Gray, to Jackson County Historical Society president Joe Rhinehart, and to Western Carolina University Special Collections director George Frizzell for their contributions toward preserving local history.*

ISBN 978-0-7385-6772-3

Library of Congress Control Number: 2009920848

Published by Arcadia Publishing
Charleston, South Carolina

Printed in the United States of America

Then and Now is a registered trademark and is used under license from Salamander Books Limited

For all general information contact Arcadia Publishing at:
Telephone 843-853-2070
Fax 843-853-0044
E-mail sales@arcadiapublishing.com

Visit us on the Internet at www.arcadiapublishing.com

On the Front Cover: Sylva's Mill Street bustles with activity around 1895 in this companion photograph to the page three image. The peaked-roof building on the right once housed the Wilson brothers' dry-goods establishment, called the Sylva Cash Store, and was later the Hanley-Morris dry-goods store. It was torn down around 1938, and the building that now contains part of the Blackrock Outdoor Company was constructed in its place. M. Buchanan's store was located to the left of the taller building. Mill Street is in the foreground, and the picture was taken near the site of the old depot, which was demolished in the late 1970s. (Then image, courtesy of Lynn Hotaling; now image, courtesy of Nick Breedlove.)

On the Back Cover: More than 3,000 people crowded into downtown Sylva for what was the biggest occasion in Jackson County's then 64-year history—the unveiling and dedication of a monument to honor Jackson County soldiers who fought for the Confederacy during the Civil War. That gathering took place on September 18, 1915. Some 80 years later, in the mid-1990s, the statue was removed, refurbished, and rededicated. (Courtesy of the *Sylva Herald*.)

Contents

Acknowledgments

This book would not have been possible without the cooperation and assistance of those who shared their cherished old photographs. Their names are listed on the pages where their photographs appear, and we thank them all. Certain individuals made extraordinary contributions, and we are honored to have had their support. Thanks to *Sylva Herald* publisher Steve Gray for his generosity in allowing publication of *Herald* file photographs; to George Frizzell, director of Special Collections at Western Carolina University's Hunter Library, for sharing his considerable knowledge and allowing us to include rare photographs from WCU's archives; to *Herald* sports editor Carey Phillips, whose grandfather started the *Ruralite*, the *Sylva Herald*'s forerunner, for research assistance and proofreading; to local historian Rachel Brown Phillips for research assistance; to John and Robin Kevlin at Metrostat for donating the use of their bucket truck to secure a modern image; to Kathleen Breedlove for viewing old photographs and proofreading; to Jeff and Matt Breedlove for general support and encouragement; to Richard Hotaling for research assistance; to Ellen Hotaling for assistance with current photographs; to Scott Hotaling for general support and encouragement; and to Elizabeth Hotaling, who proofread the final manuscript for consistency and style.

Unless otherwise noted, all the modern images were taken by Nick Breedlove.

Introduction

Jackson County, North Carolina, is defined by its lofty vistas and fast-flowing water. Carved from portions of two adjoining counties in 1851, the county encompasses some 185 named summits and approximately 250 named rivers and creeks. Within its 494 square miles, elevations range from less than 2,000 feet above sea level in Whittier's broad Tuckaseigee River valley to more than 6,000 feet on mountaintops in the Plott Balsam and Great Balsam ranges.

Notable geographic features include Richland Balsam, the county's tallest peak (at 6,410 feet), as well as the highest point along the entire Blue Ridge Parkway (at 6,053 feet); Whitewater Falls (at 411 feet), the second-highest cascade east of the Rocky Mountains; Whiteside Mountain, which boasts the highest vertical cliffs in the eastern United States; and Panthertown Valley near Cashiers, which has been described as the "Yosemite of the East."

The Tuckaseigee River flows almost the length of the county, and major roads follow the river: N.C. 107 parallels it between East LaPorte and Tuckasegee and follows its West Fork to Glenville; N.C. 281 travels alongside the river's East Fork; and U.S. 74, like the railroad tracks that preceded it, mostly follows the Tuckaseigee's path from Dillsboro to the Jackson/Swain County line. To the north, the Oconaluftee River forms part of the Jackson/Swain County line; to the south, the Whitewater and Chattooga Rivers separate Jackson from Transylvania and Macon Counties, respectively.

Jackson County includes a significant amount of U.S. National Forest land, including the 39,000-acre Roy Taylor Forest, part of the larger Nantahala National Forest, which is southwest of and adjacent to the Blue Ridge Parkway. The Taylor Forest is composed of land that formerly belonged to the Mead Corporation and includes both the Tuckaseigee Gorge and Panthertown Valley.

The parkway, which was constructed to provide a scenic link between the Shenandoah and Great Smoky Mountains National Parks, winds back and forth along the Jackson/Haywood border. A portion of the Cherokee Indian Reservation—also known by its historic name, Qualla Boundary—lies within Jackson County; the reservation borders the Great Smoky Mountains National Park.

The county's population in 2000 was 33,121, according to the U.S. Census report. It has four incorporated towns—Webster, Sylva, Dillsboro, and Forest Hills—and several other well-defined communities with post offices, including Cashiers, Glenville, Tuckasegee, Cullowhee, Balsam, and Whittier.

Jackson County is also known for its educational institutions. It is home to Western Carolina University (WCU), which began in 1889 as the Cullowhee Normal and Industrial School, grew into a major regional university, and is now a member campus of the University of North Carolina system. In addition, the county includes Southwestern Community College, a top-ranked two-year school that offers a college transfer program as well as a variety of technical degrees and certifications.

The county traces its existence back to an 1851 act of North Carolina's General Assembly. Prior to that time, the Tuckaseigee River was the dividing line between Haywood and Macon Counties, which each gave up territory to the new county. Named for Pres. Andrew Jackson, it had its first county seat at Webster, though that changed some 60 years later when Sylva became the governmental seat.

"Removalists"—those who favored moving the county seat from Webster to Sylva—first made their plea to the General Assembly in 1901, though they had been pushing the idea since around 1888. Lawmakers granted that request, but the bill was never acted upon through a local county vote. The main reasons given by those who favored the change was that Sylva had both a railroad and an economy that was starting to boom. Sylva's bright future would improve if it was also the county seat, they said. C. J. Harris, the richest man in the county, was also one of the most outspoken removalists and told Jackson County citizens he would build them a new courthouse if they would approve the move, though he stipulated that he would do so for a sum not to exceed $30,000.

William Dallas Wike of Cullowhee, who was Jackson County's representative in the 1913 session of the General Assembly, brought removal back to the floor in February. The removal debate created an intense rivalry between Sylva and Webster, and between those on both sides of the move; the issue remained hot until the day of the vote. By 10:00 p.m. on May 8, 1913, the election was over and had been conceded to the removalists. By a vote of 1,413 for removal and 738 against, Sylva became the county seat.

While most of Sylva's downtown buildings were constructed more than 60 years ago, the businesses they first housed have mostly disappeared, with grocery stores, gas stations, and dry-goods stores giving way to restaurants and specialty shops. The 1998 streetscape effort, led by the Downtown Sylva Association (then the Sylva Partners in Renewal) and funded by the Town of Sylva, added new streetlights, trees, and benches to the downtown area, rejuvenating Sylva's downtown.

CHAPTER 1

Cullowhee, Tuckasegee, and Southern Jackson

The Johns Creek School, which once stood on Caney Fork Road just past the mouth of Johns Creek, was built around 1925 and was consolidated with the Cullowhee school in 1965. The building deteriorated and was finally torn down in the early 1980s, but the school's bell has been refurbished and now hangs at the Caney Fork Community Center. (Courtesy of Jackson County Schools.)

A small crowd gathers at the Glenville Dam on October 13, 1941, to mark the completion of Nantahala Power and Light Company's (now Duke Energy's) Glenville hydroelectric project. With World War II raging in Europe, the project was completed between June 1940 and October 1941. Glenville's construction was rushed to increase the supply of electricity available to the Aluminum Company of America's plants in Alcoa, Tennessee. NP&L changed the name of the lake and powerhouse to Thorpe in the 1950s, but the Glenville name was restored to the lake and dam around 2000. (Courtesy of Fred Alexander/Duke Energy.)

The water flow over the High Falls of the Tuckaseigee River was greatly reduced with the 1941 completion of the Glenville Dam. Water from the reservoir is now piped to a powerhouse at the foot of the mountain, bypassing the falls, which were once a popular hiking destination. An early tourist publication described High Falls as "the most stupendous waterfall of the mountains." (Courtesy of Western Carolina University [WCU] Special Collections.)

Hampton Barnes pumps gas around 1950 in front of the store he operated along N.C. 107 between Tuckasegee and Glenville. According to his widow, Christine Barnes, he ran the store from 1950 until 1965. In addition to gas, he sold groceries and bait, she said. After closing the store, Hampton Barnes operated a television-repair shop in the old building until around 1990. (Courtesy of Christine Barnes.)

Work proceeds on September 9, 1953, on the crest of Nantahala Power and Light Company's Bear Creek Dam, one of four dams on the Tuckaseigee River's East Fork in Jackson County's Canada section. Construction of the 215-foot-high dam and 473-acre lake began in 1952, and the project was generating power by 1954. The power company spent some $8 million on its entire East Fork project, which includes Bear Creek, Cedar Cliff, Wolf Creek, and Tanassee Creek dams, lakes, and powerhouses. (Courtesy of Fred Alexander/Duke Energy.)

Opened in 1951 to students consolidated from Charleys Creek, Rock Bridge, Sols Creek, Tanassee Gap, and Wolf Creek schools, the four-classroom, redbrick Canada School made national headlines in March 1967 when Lady Bird Johnson, wife of then-president Lyndon Johnson, visited. Consolidated with the Cullowhee school in 1982, the Canada School stood empty for more than two decades. Ownership was transferred to Jackson County around 2002, and the building was razed in April 2004 to make way for the current community park, which was completed in late 2007. (Courtesy of the *Sylva Herald*.)

Area residents survey the results of Jackson County's greatest natural disaster, the 1940 flood, which washed out both approaches to the bridge over the Tuckaseigee River's East Fork and rendered the road impassable to vehicles; people had to use ladders to climb onto the bridge. Looking south up N.C. 107, the Tuckasegee Wesleyan Church, established in 1919, is visible on the hill in both photographs. What were termed "cloudbursts" and "waterspouts" that occurred mainly in the Canada and Caney Fork sections sent the river on a rampage, with floodwaters at Tuckasegee cresting at 21 feet, or 40,300 cubic feet per second. (Courtesy of Fred Alexander/Duke Energy.)

The Jack and Laura Wike house in Tuckasegee provides the backdrop for a mid-summer 1928 Hooper/Wike reunion. The house burned down in August of that year. Occupying the site today is the rock home of Tommy and Joann Beutell, which was built by the Wikes' son, Claude Wike. During the Great Depression, the Wikes sold their house and farm to Dr. John Brinkley, Jackson County's most notorious native son. Brinkley began treating male impotence by transplanting goat glands into aging men at hospitals he founded in Milford, Kansas, and Del Rio, Texas. (Courtesy of Frank Moody.)

John Moody, in front of his farmhouse in East LaPorte in 1918, holds his granddaughter, Genevieve Moody Nicholson; his wife, Emily Wike Moody, is on the left, and on the right is Eula Moody, wife of John and Emily's son, Leon. Standing behind John are Emily's sisters, Rhoda and Mary Wike, with Leon and Eula's daughter, Opal Lee Moody Clark. The house was built in the 1880s by Andrew and Mariah Fulbright Wike, who moved into the area from Lincoln County and had four daughters—Emily, Mary, Rhoda, and Mariah. Emily married John Moody from South Carolina; their son Leon married Eula Painter, and Leon and Eula's daughter, Opal Lee, married Tobe Clark and inherited her grandparents' house, which Clark remodeled over the years. After the Clarks' deaths, the farm passed to their son, Michael, who sold it to Legasus of North Carolina. The land development company plans a golf course and vacation homes on the property. (Courtesy of Margaret Clark.)

The Blackwood Lumber Company's sawmill, wood yard, company store, and mill houses once stood in East LaPorte near the current Sun Dog Places, a custom home builder. The company built the Tuckaseigee and Southeastern Railroad from Sylva to East LaPorte, which added passenger service beginning in 1922. By that year, Blackwood had also constructed the mill town (shown below) to house some 100 workers and their families. Those homes had electricity and indoor plumbing years before such things were common in more remote areas of Jackson County. Blackwood, which once owned some 40,000 acres extending from Scotts Creek to the Canada community, sold its property to the Mead Paper Company around 1940 and shut down its operations. (Courtesy of Sue Phillips.)

This house, built in 1910 and shown here a year later, stands on Helen Zachary Road in Caney Fork Valley. It was built by Jefferson Davis Zachary, a farmer and merchant, whose holdings at one time totaled several hundred acres. Zachary's wife, Susie Jane Potts Zachary, was one of the first graduates of the Cullowhee Normal School, earning her degree in 1891. (Courtesy of Sue Phillips.)

The Robert Slagle Green house on Caney Fork belonged to Green and his wife, Sally Hunter Green, who ran a small general store there from around 1906 until the mid-1970s. They also had a mill, which was attached to the store, where they ground corn, and they offered a shoe-repair service in addition to selling groceries and dry goods. R. S. Green died in 1948, and Sally and their son Dan continued to operate the store for another 25 years or so. (Courtesy of Judy Harrell.)

John Nelson Hunter built this home on Caney Fork around 1887. He and his second wife, Emily, sit in front of the house around 1914; with them are Elizabeth (child) and Stella Brown. Hunter's first wife, Minerva, who had consumption, returned to Jackson County from Texas in 1887 because it was thought that the mountain air would cure her. She died that same year, and Hunter married her sister Emily. Hunter's great-granddaughter, present owner Judy Harrell, has remodeled the house and now makes her home there. (Courtesy of Judy Harrell.)

Judaculla Rock, located near Caney Fork Creek, is a soapstone petroglyph once owned by the Parker family. During the 1930s, the rock was painted to bring out the details of the ancient Native American writing; the meaning of the symbols remains unknown. J. B. Parker donated the site to Jackson County around 1960, and an effort is now under way to protect this important archaeological site and add a greenway. (Courtesy of WCU Special Collections.)

Students line up around 1905 in front of the one-time Norton School, which is now the Norton Community Center. Little information is available about the school, though it still existed in county records in 1913. Land for the school was donated by Samuel Logan McGuire, grandfather of Dr. Patsy McGuire of Sylva. The school was later moved to a new location to accommodate road construction and ended up back on McGuire land. By the time the county had consolidated schools and decided to tear the structure down, Dr. Wayne McGuire (Patsy's father) had inherited the property and would not let it be demolished. From the time the school moved out, the building was used by various community organizations and, at times, has been used for church services, according to Patsy McGuire, who inherited the property from her father and donated it to Jackson County around 1985. (Courtesy of Patsy McGuire.)

The old Gola and Jerdie Ferguson house stood in 1973 on the present-day Cullowhee Valley School campus, near the back entrance bridge. After standing empty for some 15 years, the house was moved across Speedwell Road in the late 1970s to make way for the relocation of N.C. 107. The house belonged to a Western Carolina University (WCU) fraternity before being purchased in 2003 by Jack Debnam for the Cullowhee office of Western Carolina Properties. (Courtesy of Lynn Hotaling.)

The concrete bridge at Cullowhee was destroyed by the flood of August 30, 1940, as was every other bridge across the main Tuckaseigee River in Jackson County. Buildings in the background are, from left to right, Robert Brown's house, Brown's store, and Battle's Grocery, which also housed the Cullowhee Post Office. The old railroad line from Sylva to East LaPorte is visible in front of Battle's, as is the smokestack at the steam plant on Western Carolina University's campus. To the right of the smokestack is the Cullowhee Baptist Church Cemetery. The top of the smokestack is still barely visible above the trees, and a few of the cemetery's markers can be seen to the left of the power line. The buildings that once housed both Brown's house and store still stand, though they have been remodeled over the years. (Courtesy of the *Sylva Herald*.)

The Cullowhee Dam, seen here during the 1920s but before 1928, when the power plant was moved to the opposite side of the Tuckaseigee River, was initially made of logs and washed away in 1926 and 1928. What was then Western Carolina College began generating electricity around 1918 and initially used the same turbine that powered the gristmill in the older photograph to turn its generator. The concrete dam that currently impounds the river was completed in 1930 and was built by Biltmore Concrete Company along with a powerhouse that generated power both for Western Carolina University (WCU) and its surrounding community. Electricity is no longer produced at the site, though WCU continued to generate power there into the 1960s. The dam retains its importance, however, because the intakes for both the university water-treatment plant, completed in 1966, and the county water-treatment plant, completed in 1997, are located just upstream of the dam. (Courtesy of WCU Special Collections.)

Jackson County's oldest church, Cullowhee Baptist, looked quite different in the early 1920s. The white frame structure was constructed around 1918 and was located in front of the church cemetery between the present-day brick sanctuary and Baptist Student Union. Cullowhee Baptist organized in 1821 near Webster as Unity Baptist Church. The congregation moved to a log building at the mouth of Cullowhee Creek in 1830, and the church's name was changed to Cullowhee Baptist sometime during that decade. In 1865, the congregation moved to higher ground near the church cemetery, adjacent to what is now Western Carolina University, and moved into the present church in 1930. (Courtesy of WCU Special Collections.)

This *c.* 1928 view from Buzzard's Roost comprises what then was the entire Western Carolina University (WCU) campus. Buildings visible include, from left to right, the old Cullowhee Baptist Church; the original Madison Building; the old heating plant; the Davies Home; the Music and Art Building (shortly before it was torn down); the Joyner building; the nearly completed Moore Dormitory; and the Cullowhee Methodist Church, which was then located where Breese gymnasium stands today. In the foreground is part of the "Town House" farm, secured by WCU in 1924 after the death of Dave Rogers. The recent photograph includes the steeple of present-day Cullowhee Baptist, with the second Madison Building, completed in 1939 on the site of the first, just to the right of the steeple. The foreground is taken up by the Hunter Library and the Natural Sciences Building, two of several WCU facilities constructed on the old Rogers farm. (Courtesy of WCU Special Collections.)

Western Carolina University's Stillwell Science Building (left) and the Hunter Library, nearing completion (below) in 1952, are two of the buildings constructed during WCU's second major expansion period, which occurred in the early 1950s. The library, completed in 1953 and named for longtime president Hiram T. Hunter, was the first WCU facility built as a library; prior to its construction, the library shared the Joyner Building with several other departments. When a major addition to the Hunter Library was dedicated in March 1967, Lady Bird Johnson, wife of Pres. Lyndon B. Johnson, was on hand for the event. The library was completely renovated during the early 1980s, and the "new" Hunter Library was dedicated in April 1983. (Courtesy of WCU Special Collections.)

The Stillwell Science Building is named for longtime professor Edgar H. Stillwell. In the photograph below, taken when the building was completed in 1952, the right wing is still two floors high. A third story was added to that part of the structure in 1959, and the Stillwell building recently received a complete makeover and modernization, including a revamped front, through funding approved by a 2002 North Carolina education bond referendum. (Courtesy of WCU Special Collections.)

Western Carolina University's Hoey Auditorium, named for Clyde Hoey, North Carolina's governor from 1937 until 1941, is shown here (above) in 1939, the year it was dedicated. Construction of the 900-seat auditorium was part of a six-building expansion, which included the Breese, McKee, Graham, "new" Madison, and "old" Student Union buildings, and virtually doubled the size of the Cullowhee campus. The building was closed for renovations during 1988 and reopened in 1989, boasting a modern theater. (Courtesy of WCU Special Collections.)

On his way to winning a 2-mile race in Cullowhee in 1974, West Georgia runner Jim Gaines saw a different landscape than the one that now surrounds Western Carolina University's track. N.C. 107 had not been relocated to the northwest end of campus where it runs today (visible in the background of the photograph below), and Long Branch Road (now Little Savannah Road) began on campus. Runners in the early 1970s also lacked a field house (on the right in the recent photograph), which was added in 2005 when the track was resurfaced. (Courtesy of Lynn Hotaling.)

CHAPTER 2

Dillsboro, Webster, and Northern Jackson

Webster's two-story, 20-room Mountain View Hotel was lost in a spectacular fire on November 13, 1910. The fire started in the hotel's kitchen; with no organized fire departments, bucket brigades were the only means of battling the blaze. Also lost to that same fire was the 10-room Nathan Coward boardinghouse and the Webster Pharmacy on one side of the street and the Tuckaseigee Bank building and the Andy Allison residence on the other. Flames were checked in time to save the post office. (Courtesy of Betty Coward Stillwell.)

Built in 1914 by early Jackson County entrepreneur C. J. Harris to provide power for his Harris-Rees Tannery and to light the streets of Dillsboro and Sylva, the Dillsboro Dam was acquired by Nantahala Power and Light (NP&L) in 1957, when NP&L bought the Dillsboro and Sylva Electric Company. The dam is now owned by Duke Energy, which bought NP&L in 1988. The dam and power plant have been in the news for the past several years because of a proposal by Duke that would remove the 93-year-old dam as part of a mitigation package for new licenses it is seeking from the Federal Energy Regulatory Commission for its other hydroelectric projects in Jackson County. (Courtesy of National Archives.)

Dillsboro's streets were covered with water in the wake of flooding in April 1964 (pictured above). The village, which traces its roots back to 1883 and was chartered in 1889, is named in honor of William Allen Dills. The modern image reveals a much "greener" Dillsboro, with the trees that have grown up obscuring many landmarks, including the Jarrett Memorial Baptist Church steeple (top left in the above photograph) and present-day Dogwood Crafters (the log structure at middle left above and barely visible through the leaves in the recent image). Webster Street still crosses the railroad tracks in the same spot. (Courtesy of the *Sylva Herald*.)

Looking up Dillsboro's Webster Street around 1930, the 100-plus-year-old Jarrett House took center stage, as it still does today. Constructed around 1884 by Dillsboro founder William Allen Dills, the Jarrett House (center in both photographs) was originally named the Mount Beulah Hotel. It was purchased from Dills in 1894 by Robert Jarrett and renamed the Jarrett Springs Hotel after the new owner and a sulfur spring once located behind the hotel. Today the Jarrett House is owned by Jim and Jean Hartbarger. The sign on the right corner in the above photograph reads, "Asheville 54 miles; Murphy 72 miles." (Courtesy of Peggy Mason.)

The Cannon Brothers Gas and Oil Company, pictured below in the late 1960s, operated in Dillsboro until the mid-1980s, when Jim Cannon sold the business to Morgan Oil. Cannon Brothers began in 1913 as a general store in Dillsboro and grew to become the Shell Oil distributors for western North Carolina. The building served as the arrival and departure point for the Great Smoky Mountains Railroad's Dillsboro excursion trains until 2008. (Courtesy of the *Sylva Herald*.)

The Tuckaseigee River looks different these days than it did around 1909 prior to construction of the Dillsboro Dam, which was built by early industrialist C. J. Harris around 1913. The building on the right closest to the river (in the vintage photograph) is believed to be an old ice plant and is thought to have been located approximately where Dillsboro's town park is now. The bridge that is visible in the photograph below was just above the confluence of Scotts Creek and the Tuckaseigee, which means it was downstream of the present-day highway bridge. (Courtesy of the *Sylva Herald*.)

The Savannah Elementary School, built by the Works Progress Administration, opened in the fall of 1941. It consolidated four smaller schools—Zion Hill, Gay, East Fork, and Greens Creek. Viewpoint, the fifth school in the district, had merged with Gay two years before when the Viewpoint building was destroyed by fire. Savannah ceased to be used as a school following the 1972–1973 school year, when it was consolidated with Webster and Sylva Elementary Schools to form Fairview. The Old School Antique Mall has operated in the former school since the late 1970s. (Courtesy of Jackson County Schools.)

The East Fork home of Lorenzo Dow and Lillie Ann Hall, pictured above around 1910, was built around 1900. In the photograph are Dow and Lillie Hall and their children and first grandchild. The house is now the home of Jim and Melissa Zoda, who purchased the property about 10 years ago from Bryant Cowan, one of the Halls' grandchildren. (Courtesy of Ruth Ashe.)

Looking south toward Franklin just past the intersection of N.C. 116 and U.S. 441 around 1930, a Ford Model T travels through a different landscape than is visible in the same location today. Country Road Farms nursery is to the left of the modern highway that now connects Dillsboro and Franklin. Today's four-lane road was completed during the mid-1970s with federal funds funneled into Jackson County by the Appalachian Regional Commission. (Courtesy of the *Sylva Herald*.)

This *c.* 1925 view of the "Barkers Creek Straight" on U.S. 74/441 was taken looking west from what was then Highway 10 and shows the S. C. Allison farm. Several of those buildings are still standing and have been incorporated into the modern commercial enterprises lining the four-lane highway that now connects Sylva with Cherokee, Bryson City, and the Great Smoky Mountains National Park. (Courtesy of the *Sylva Herald*.)

The N.C. National Guard Armory was almost completed in November 1964. Construction began in June of that year, and the structure cost $147,486.26, of which Jackson County paid $24,841.98. The road in the left background leads to the then-new Jackson County Industrial Education Center, which is now known as Southwestern Community College. (Courtesy of the *Sylva Herald*.)

Webster Baptist Church has not changed much during the past 80 or so years, as witnessed by the fact that the 1930 photograph is remarkably similar to the recent picture (below). Located on N.C. 116, the church is listed on the National Register of Historic Places. Founded in 1854, the church moved to its present-day location in May 1900. (Courtesy of Jim McGinnis.)

Webster's frame school building, which opened to students in 1906, stood on N.C. 116 just left of the rock school that replaced it in 1937 and is visible at right in the recent photograph. The old school had a gymnasium on the second floor and a metal, spiral fire escape at the back of the school. The rock building now houses the Southwestern Child Development Commission, the Webster Child Development Center, and the Family Resource Center. (Courtesy of Jim McGinnis.)

The Webster School, completed by the Works Progress Administration in 1937, still stands on N.C. 116. It housed all of Webster's schoolchildren until 1960, when Webster's high school was consolidated with Sylva's to form Sylva-Webster High. The rock building continued as an elementary school until the 1973–1974 school year. (Courtesy of Jackson County Schools.)

This garage still stands at the old William Tyler Buchanan home place on Buchanan Loop in Webster. The two men in the 1940s photograph are William Julian McElhinney (left), who married William Tyler's daughter, Ruby Louise Buchanan; and his namesake, Julian McElhinney Buchanan, grandson of William Tyler and son of Roy Glenn Buchanan. The driver is unidentified. (Courtesy of Jim McGinnis.)

Constructed in 1887–1888 at a cost of $12,000, the second Webster Courthouse stood at the corner of N.C. 116 and Buchanan Loop where the Rhinehart home now stands. It served as the county's governmental center from 1888 until 1913, when voters passed a referendum that moved the county seat to Sylva. The county then sold the property, and Joseph and Lily Cagle Rhinehart, grandparents of present owner Joe Rhinehart, bought the old courthouse and the land it stood on in the 1930s from the original purchaser. All that was left of the courthouse was the tower, and the Rhineharts tore that down and built their home from its bricks. Webster's first courthouse, which was torn down to make way for the second one, also stood on this site. (Courtesy of Joe Rhinehart.)

CHAPTER 3

Sylva and Surroundings

The old Sylva Graded School once stood near city hall in the area where the town swimming pool is located today. After Sylva High School's 1924 opening in what would become Mark Watson Park, the graded school housed the town's elementary school until 1929, when a new elementary school was constructed near the high school. (Courtesy of WCU Special Collections.)

The area that now comprises Mark Watson Park—the former Jackson County Fairgrounds that was once known as "Baum Bottom"—was first home to the county's annual agricultural fairs and then to Sylva's elementary and high schools. The first fair was held in 1908 on College Hill but was moved to Baum Bottom the following year. After the 1909 fair, the Jackson County Fair Association incorporated and bought part of Baum Bottom and built grandstands, exhibition buildings, and stalls. The 1924 opening of Sylva High School, which was located to the right of the tent in the photograph below until it was torn down in 1990, ended the fairs. (Courtesy of Rachel Phillips.)

Members of the 1956 Sylva High School (SHS) homecoming court smile for the camera during that year's homecoming parade and again during the SHS class of 1957's 50th reunion. The winner was Betsy Crawford (Goldtrap) of Mount Pleasant, South Carolina, who is on the right in both photographs. With Crawford in 1957 and 2007 are, from left to right, Tommye Bradley (Saunooke) of Cherokee and Love Brendle (Wooten) of Chappaqua, New York. (Both courtesy of J. D. Patterson.)

A Sylva Armistice Day parade rounds the curve at the west end of town around 1920. The two buildings behind the floats are Early's Service Station (left), thought to be run by Sion Early, and Osborne Buchanan's barn. The west end of Main Street was reconfigured in 1998 as part of the streetscape construction. (Courtesy of the *Sylva Herald*.)

The Citizens Bank and Trust Company opened in February 1963 with Jennings Bryson as manager. Citizens merged with Wachovia Bank and Trust of Winston-Salem in 1970, and the bank on the corner of Main and Schulman Streets became a branch of Wachovia. Through the years, the building has undergone extensive renovations, including the addition of second-floor office space. (Courtesy of the *Sylva Herald*.)

Allison's car dealership was still located on Main Street in the former Sears Building when the photograph below was snapped in 1959 for a newspaper advertisement. Published in the *Sylva Herald*'s May 21, 1959, issue, the advertisement told of the dealer's "redecorated" display lot and "protractive" cover that protected its new cars rain or shine. Dan Allison's automotive and appliance business was initially located in the *Sylva Herald* building and moved to the west end of Main Street in the late 1940s. New cars on display in the spring of 1959 included an Oldsmobile, a Jeep, a Studebaker, and a Rambler. Allison's, now a Chevrolet dealer, moved to its current location west of downtown in the late 1960s or early 1970s. Sears moved into the Main Street building during the early 1970s and remained for more than two decades. Several short-lived businesses occupied the space before the It's By Nature gallery opened there in 2003. (Courtesy of the *Sylva Herald*.)

In 1951, Jackson County was preparing for a weeklong celebration of its centennial, as this banner across Main Street proclaims. Parked cars on the left-hand side of the street are facing the courthouse, as two-way traffic would continue on the thoroughfare for another five years. Restaurants continue to be a vital part of downtown, but gone are the gas stations, drugstores, and variety stores that once thrived in the central business district. Maple trees and benches, added as part of the 1998 streetscape project, are prominent in the recent image. (Courtesy of the *Sylva Herald*.)

A group of area residents posed in front of the Jackson Savings and Loan when the bank opened in 1958 or 1959. They include, from left to right, (first row) Lloyd Cowan, W. C. Hennessee, Tom Clayton, Dick Sellers, Joe Sellers, Bob Jackson, and Bob Parker; (second row) Eddie Queen, Mary Cowan, Bjorn "Johnny" Ahlin, Lou Bryson, Martie Franklin, Jean Franklin, Linda Barnes, Burt Wilkey, Peggy Parker, Pete Davis, Dick Green, Wayne Wilson, Andy Wilson, Clyde Franklin, Bert Lloyd, Bob Barefoot, and Bea Wall. The boy at right is thought to be a Messer, but his first name is unknown. Jay Ball opened his Jewelry Outlet there in 1987. (Courtesy of the *Sylva Herald*.)

The home of E. L. and Gertrude Dills McKee was located on the corner of Main and Landis Streets where the First Baptist Church stands today. One of Jackson County's prominent civic and industrial leaders, E. L. McKee was instrumental in the formation of the Sylva Paperboard (now Jackson Paper). His greatest legacy is probably High Hampton Inn in Cashiers, which is now owned and operated by his grandson Will McKee. Gertrude Dills McKee, daughter of Dillsboro founder William Allen Dills, was the first woman elected to serve in the North Carolina Senate. Baptists bought the property in 1952 and, in 1958, constructed an educational building before the house was demolished to make way for the sanctuary, which was completed in 1965. The large copper beech, prominent in the above photograph, is also visible in the older photograph. (Courtesy of the *Sylva Herald*.)

The Jackson County Bank, pictured below before two-way traffic on Main Street was eliminated in 1956, began in Webster in October 1905, according to *The History of Jackson County*. Sylva industrialist C. J. Harris was the first president, and before the mid-1920s, when the above building was built, the bank had moved to Sylva and was located for a time in Harris's Sylva Supply building (now Jackson's General Store). In 1954, the Jackson County Bank merged with the statewide First Union National Bank. The First Union name vanished in February 2002 when First Union bought out Wachovia but chose to operate as Wachovia. Bank officials sold Sylva's First Union branch to the Central Carolina Bank. SunTrust, which currently occupies the old Jackson County Bank building, bought out Central Carolina Bank in 2004. (Courtesy of the *Sylva Herald*.)

The old Sylva First Baptist Church that once stood in part of what is now the SunTrust Bank parking lot was torn down around 1972 after the church, which was established in 1887, built an educational building (1958) and then a sanctuary (1965) across Landis (then Walnut) Street. The above sanctuary and educational building were built in 1908 and 1938, respectively. Also visible is the corner of a building that once housed the Central Shell Station, operated by Maude and Polk Allman from around 1958 through 1971. Traffic was still two-way on what was then Walnut Street; the change to one-way traffic on what is now Landis Street came in early 2005. (Courtesy of the *Sylva Herald*.)

The Commercial Hotel, described in *The History of Jackson County* as a "new, two-story, up-to-date building," burned to the ground on April 6, 1923. Owned by the Hastings family, it was located on the corner of Main and Spring Streets on the site of the present-day First Citizens Bank parking lot. The fire also destroyed the Medford Furniture Company, Zachary's Barber Shop, and a nearby home. The fire's intense heat broke plate-glass windows on the opposite side of Main Street. The Manus Hanley and Mary Jane Long Morris house (see page 72) is visible at left in the above photograph. (Courtesy of June Bess Anderson.)

The Leader, a clothing store once operated on Main Street by Ben Lessing, is pictured below during the late 1950s. Hal Dennis, who, in 1965, opened Dennis Men's Store next door in the space once occupied by Frank Fricks's men's clothing store, expanded into the Leader space with his Ladies Store after the Leader closed. The building now houses one half of the Blackrock Outdoor Company, which opened in December 1999. (Courtesy of the *Sylva Herald*.)

In this 1918 view of Main Street, the first building on the left is the Commercial Hotel, which burned to the ground in 1923 and once stood in the present-day First Citizens Bank parking lot. Extending out toward the street from the hotel was Zachary's Barber Shop, where the fire was believed to have started. The First Citizens building (used to house the Tuckaseigee Bank) was constructed after the fire. (Courtesy of the *Sylva Herald*.)

The former McGuire Building that now houses the *Sylva Herald* was home to Dan Allison's auto and appliance business in 1941. After Allison's moved in the late 1940s, downstairs tenants included Elsie Massie's dress shop, which closed in 1980. The McGuires then moved their dental practice from the upper stories into the first-floor offices, where they stayed for about a decade until completion of their current building on King Street. Lawyers' offices occupied the space until the newspaper purchased the building and expanded into it in 1997. Allison's employees in the photograph above are driver Lonnie Jones and Earl Norton. (Courtesy of Daniel Allison.)

In this 1895 view of Main Street, the prominent wooden structure with the peaked roof was located to the right of the present-day Jackson's General Store, which is the brick peaked-roof building visible in the photograph below. The wooden building, which was torn down around 1938, housed the Wilson brothers' Sylva Cash Store and later the Hanley-Morris dry-goods store and Stovall's Café. In the photograph above, M. Buchanan's store is to the right of the taller wooden structure. In the photograph below, the roof of the City Lights Bookstore is in the foreground. Main Street businesses on the *Sylva Herald* side of the street include, from left to right, Massie Furniture, In Your Ear, Advanced Home Care, the former Bear Lake Reserve sales office, Restaurant 553's courtyard, and the *Sylva Herald*. Those opposite include Hollifield Jewelers, Lily's Treatures, Jackson's General Store, Blackrock Outdoor Company, Ironstone Grill, and Motion Makers. In the background, the town of Sylva's Roscoe Poteet Pool, town hall, and police station can be seen. (Courtesy of Lynn Hotaling.)

Local residents poured into a flag-draped downtown on July 4, 2006, but they did not approach the crowd that packed Main Street on September 9, 1936, to welcome Pres. Franklin D. Roosevelt, who can be seen in the backseat of the first car, waving his hat to the crowd. All of the buildings visible in the older view are still standing except for the one that housed Stovall's Café, which was then located to the right of the C. J. Harris Building (now Jackson's General Store). The Harris building, constructed around 1903, housed the Sylva Supply Company for some 95 years until that business closed in June 1999; Jackson's General Store opened four months later. The Stovall building was torn down around 1938 and was replaced by a new building for the café, and that structure is now part of the Blackrock Outdoor Company. The taller building that now makes up the other half of Blackrock once housed the clothing store the Leader. (Courtesy of WCU Special Collections.)

The house that once stood on Main Street where the Elsie Massie home stands today is pictured below during the 1890s, when the house belonged to Marcellus Sr. and Belle Buchanan, and was operated as a boardinghouse. Though it is not known precisely when the Buchanan house was torn down, it is believed that the current structure was built around 1925. (Courtesy of Elsie Massie.)

Looking west down Main Street during the mid-1950s, downtown shops across from the *Sylva Herald* offices included Jackson Furniture (right) and Schulman's Department Store. The Jackson Furniture building later housed Livingston's Photo and is still part of Livingston Kelley's photograph and framing operation. The Penumbra Gallery recently moved into the former Schulman's location. (Courtesy of the *Sylva Herald*.)

Local car dealers, from left to right, Woody Hampton with a Ford, Ray Cogdill with a Dodge, and Homer Davis with a Chevrolet, stand in front of Sossamon's Furniture Company on Main Street in 1955. According to Boyd Sossamon, who owned and operated Sossamon's from 1944 until about 1998, he needed three trucks for his business and decided to buy one of each. Cogdill owned Cogdill Motors, which at that time was just down Main Street from Sossamon's. Hampton owned Reece-Hampton Ford, later Cagle and Son, located where Rite-Aid is now. Davis was co-owner of Kirk-Davis Chevrolet, which occupied the building where P&M Automotive is today. Sossamon moved his store a few doors west around 1990 (the current Used Bookstore) for a couple of years and was on Mill Street the last few years he was in business. Jones Country Store and Main Design are currently located in the former Sossamon's. Western Auto closed in 1989; Yesterday's Tree with Shannon Berrey Designs and Dodie's Auction currently occupy its former location. (Courtesy of the *Sylva Herald*.)

Cornelius Buchanan and his wife, Katie Keen Buchanan, built this Cowan Street home in 1894. J. W. McKee bought the house in 1909 from Cornelius Buchanan. McKee's wife, Carrie, and daughter, Dorothy, then sold the house to Charlie Allison in 1923. Hattie Hilda Allison moved into the house in 1957 when she married Charlie Allison's son Edwin, and the couple lived there for 20 years before moving into a new house they built directly across Cowan Street. Dr. Clay Smallwood and his wife, Katherine, purchased the house in June 1984 and restored and renovated the century-old structure. (Courtesy of the Town of Sylva.)

The Manus Hanley and Mary Jane Long Morris house was located on the corner of Jackson and King Streets in a portion of the present-day Sylva First Methodist Church parking lot. Manus Morris sold the house to Dr. Ralph Morgan around 1970, and it was subsequently demolished to create parking space for Morgan's medical office, which was then located at the corner of Spring and Jackson Streets in the current City Lights Bookstore location. The Morrises initially owned and operated the Commercial Hotel, which is pictured on page 62. (Courtesy of Jack Morris.)

Sylva's police department is now housed in the original home of the Sylva Fire Department, which was founded in 1899 by A. J. Dills. The building was built in 1927 and initially served as both firehouse and city hall. Early firefighters included, from left to right, Charlie Price, A. J. Dills, Gordon Dillard, Roscoe Dills, Dick Wilson, ? Eckenrod, Felix Picklesimer, Paul Womack, David Dills, Theodore Mashburn, E. O. Mashburn, and D. M. Tallent. The department's second fire station, completed next door in 1960, was remodeled for Sylva's town hall after the fire department moved into its present quarters in 1980. (Courtesy of Lynn Hotaling.)

When the Sylva Swimming Pool opened on June 1, 1937, it was the only municipally owned pool west of Asheville. Bathing suits rented for 10¢ each in those days. Glen Frady was the first lifeguard, and Jack Allison was in charge of the shop (a concession stand) at the entrance to the pool. Built during the Depression by the Works Progress Administration, the old pool was torn down in 1969 to make way for Sylva's Roscoe Poteet Pool, which is currently managed by the Jackson County Recreation and Parks Department. Extensive renovations to the swimming pool were completed in 2001. (Courtesy of the *Sylva Herald*.)

Employees line up in front of the old Sylva Laundry around 1950. Floyd Patterson, whose head is between the words "Sylva" and "Laundry," was manager of the business at that time. Owner Harry Ferguson is on the far right, and the laundry's bookkeeper, J. T. Gribble, is second from right. J. D. Patterson, Floyd's son, remembers that the telephone number there was 25J. The LifeWay Community Church (the former Sylva Coal and Lumber Company) now extends into the space once occupied by the laundry. Most of the old laundry was located on *Sylva Herald* owner Jim Gray's Railroad Avenue lot, which is adjacent to Sylva's municipal parking area. (Courtesy of J. D. Patterson.)

Railroad workers are hard at work repairing damage to a downtown section of track caused by the 1940 flood. In the photograph below, the second building on the left (the telephone pole is centered on it) housed the Asheville Mica Company, and the next building past it is the old Sylva Depot. Buildings on the left in the photograph above are the Pet Stop (left) and Ward's Plumbing and Heating Company; buildings on the right are the former Hooper Builders Supply (right) and the LifeWay Community Church. The courthouse cupola is visible in the distance in both photographs. (Courtesy of the *Sylva Herald*.)

Sylva's former train depot stood on Mill Street in the geographic center of the original octagon-shaped town limits and served passenger traffic from the 1890s until 1948. The above photograph shows a crowd waiting at the depot in the early 1900s; the image was taken sometime after 1902 because the peak of the former Sylva Supply Company (now Jackson's General Store), which was built in that year, is visible in the background. With the demolition of the depot during the late 1970s, the back of the Sylva Supply building can be seen clearly from the train tracks. The concrete platform where the depot once stood is now used for parking. A surveyors' mark indicating the exact center of town is still visible. (Courtesy of Claude Jones.)

The Mead Corporation published the above photograph that shows the proposed relocation of the highway and Scotts Creek near the paper company in the April 1954 edition of the *Sylvan*, a publication of Mead's Sylva plant. Lawrence Monteith's store was in the vicinity of where the Valero station is today. Visible in the upper center of the older photograph is the Raymond Nicholson residence, which is still standing but is obscured by trees in the recent image. The relocation of the road and creek allowed Mead to add a 100-foot extension to its building. (Courtesy of Hattie Hilda Allison.)

Jack Allison's tire store, located across from the Coffee Shop, was a thriving business in the mid-1950s, when the photograph below is believed to have been taken. Allison (right) sold the establishment in 1971 to current owner Paul Hall, who has worked at the tire company since he was 15 with the exception of his military service. Hall, who still operates Hall's Tire Service, said he cannot remember when the shed at right was torn down. These days, Hall said, he mostly repairs smaller tires, such as those used on lawn mowers and wheelbarrows. Hall still uses a tire-welder that is a holdover from Allison's and said he thinks it is one of only a few still in use. (Courtesy of the *Sylva Herald*.)

The intersection of East Main Street and Chipper Curve Road looked like this in 1930, when Chipper Curve Road was the main highway into Sylva from the east and was designated as U.S. 19-23 and N.C. 10. One structure visible in both photographs is the house above the Coffee Shop, then the home of Frank and Mayme Bailey. The original Coffee Shop, located just west of the current restaurant, is visible, as is the home of Mayme's parents, Roland and Sallie Painter, which stood west of the old Coffee Shop. A highway sign indicates traffic should turn left for N.C. 106, which went toward Cullowhee. A signs in the photograph below says "N. C. Law Stop," apparently referring to the railroad crossing. As the current photographs (above and on page 81) show, that crossing was relocated slightly to the east in the 1960s. (Courtesy of Tim Barker/North Carolina Department of Transportation.)

This view of the Chipper Curve Road intersection shows highway signs for left turns across the railroad tracks on U.S. 19-23 and N.C. 10, with a right turn indicated for N.C. 106. The building that now houses Hall's Tire Service (left) then appears to have been a Chevrolet dealership and a Standard gasoline station. The building now housing the WSG Bath and Lighting Gallery (left in page 80 photograph and right in this page's photograph) has a "motor company" sign, possibly B&T, on it. The above photograph shows smoke coming from a smokestack at the tannery, then known as the Armour Leather Company. (Courtesy of Tim Barker/North Carolina Department of Transportation.)

The Coffee Shop on West Main Street is Sylva's oldest restaurant. The business was established in 1926 by Roland Painter and his daughter, Mayme Bailey. The current building was constructed in 1955 after the original structure was torn down. The sign on the right indicates the building was air-conditioned, a rarity in Sylva at that time. Curb service was offered in those days. Present owner Gary Gibson bought the business from Bill Collins in 1986 and has gradually remodeled the building, with the most recent renovations completed around 2003. (Courtesy of the *Sylva Herald*.)

The Great Atlantic and Pacific Tea Company (A&P), which opened downtown across from the *Sylva Herald* around 1926, moved to this location in 1956. The local A&P moved to a much-larger building at Sylva Plaza in 1978, and the Family Dollar store moved into the building after the grocery store's departure. Sylva's A&P closed for good in January 1998 after more than seven decades in the town; Sav-Mor is now open in the A&P's former Sylva Plaza location. (Courtesy of the *Sylva Herald*.)

The Carolina Tire Company opened in Sylva in 1966, when the photograph below was taken, and continued its Main Street operation for more than 30 years, closing in the late 1990s. A similar company occupied the building briefly, and Haywood Builders Supply remodeled and refurbished the structure before opening the Design Center around 2003. (Courtesy of the *Sylva Herald*.)

The old Sylva Tannery was completed around 1900. Founded by C. J. Harris, the tannery was called by different names—Harris-Rees, Harris, Sylva, and Parsons—and was located by Scotts Creek in East Sylva. Armour Leather bought the tannery in 1915. Armour ceased operation in 1957 and sold its property to the adjoining Mead Corporation plant, which had opened in 1928. Mead closed in 1974, and the plant reopened as Jackson Paper (in the foreground in the photograph below) around 1981. (Courtesy of Claude Jones.)

The old F&P Supermarket building was still standing beside N.C. 107 across from Cody's in the 1980s, though the grocery store had by then been replaced by the Bargain Place and Queen's Discount Shoes. The structure was torn down around 2001 to make room for the Macon Bank and its parking lot, according to Padgett McCoy, who started the F&P in 1957 with his brother Furman. Furman McCoy pulled out after a year, and Padgett McCoy continued to operate the store, which was known for its quality meats, through 1977. Ray Bennett bought the business from Padgett McCoy and operated a grocery store under the F&P name for another five or six years. Cody's is visible on the left in both photographs, though the building in the above photograph was torn down in 1998 to make way for the present-day station. The building that used to be Clark's Auto Parts, then Smokey Mountain Video, and now houses Blossman Gas and Shake Healthy, can be seen on the right side of the road in both pictures as well. (Courtesy of Lana Phillips.)

The four-way intersection of N.C. 107 and Cope Creek and Walter Ashe Roads was less hurried in 1956, not long after Clarence Cody opened his service station. The building in the foreground is the original station, which was torn down in 1967 to make way for four lanes on N.C. 107. Cody's second building was torn down in 1998 to make way for the present-day station, operated by Steve Cody, Clarence Cody's son. Across the road is Clark's Auto Parts, opened by Cash Clark in 1949. Clark was joined in that business in 1980 by his son-in-law, Arthur Phillips, who continued the operation after Clark's 1988 death. Homer Holden's mother had a cloth shop on the Walter Ashe Road side of the building for a time, and subsequent businesses there included a restaurant and the Tuckaseigee Mills outlet before John Forrest moved his Smokey Mountain Video operation there around 1993. The building now houses Blossman Gas. One house visible in the 1950s photograph, the second on the right up Walter Ashe Road, is still standing, though it has been remodeled. The Macon Bank and its parking lot now occupy the other corner of Walter Ashe Road and N.C. 107, replacing the old F&P Supermarket and the house and shop building that were there in 1956. (Courtesy of Steve Cody.)

The Sylva-Webster High School, now known as Smoky Mountain High, was almost ready for occupancy when the photograph below was taken. The school opened in the fall of 1960 with the consolidation of Sylva High and Webster High, and its name was changed to Smoky Mountain High when Sylva-Webster and the Cullowhee school consolidated in 1988. The main building looked almost the same as it did in 1960 until renovations began around 2003. The gym is still almost identical, with the exception of new windows put in around 2005 and a small addition on the side. While work on what was to become the baseball field was still under way at the time of the early picture, the home side of the football stadium and the original press box had already been built. (Courtesy of the *Sylva Herald*.)

These views were taken from the hill behind Terry's Produce. Looking north toward the present-day location of McDonald's and Food Lion, the above image (taken around 1930) shows growth beginning in the area. The Raymond Nicholson home (left foreground) is still visible through the trees in the photograph below, as is the John Wilson house, which still stands behind Performance Motors. Much has changed in the recent photograph, including the construction of Eckerd's (now Rite-Aid), the Asheville Highway (Business 23), the Skyland Care Center on the hill behind McDonald's, and Wayne Smith's Bridge Street trailer park (center left). (Courtesy of the *Sylva Herald*.)

Drivers line up by their trucks at the Bunny Bread Company, which was located on Skyland Drive until about 1991. The building was constructed around 1966, according to Bill Lewis, who purchased the structure in December 1993 and opened Bill's Quick Lube in May 1994. Drivers, from left to right, are Frank Hooper, Ray Gibby, James Carpenter, James Beasley, and Charles McConnell Sr. It is likely that the above photograph was taken around 1966, when the Bunny Bread Company opened its Sylva operation. (Courtesy of the *Sylva Herald*.)

Knight's Store in Balsam survived a March 22, 1954, fire that destroyed the building behind it, which at that time contained the Balsam Post Office and a store operated by S. A. Futrel on the ground level and an apartment occupied by the Roy Saunders family on the second floor. Firefighters from Sylva, Hazelwood, and Waynesville saved the store's ice cream box and the money from the post office, but the building was a total loss. According to the *Sylva Herald*'s March 25, 1954, edition, Futrel's losses totaled $10,000, and the Saunderses' lost property was valued at $3,500. A Sylva fire truck is nearest the burning building, with trucks from Hazelwood and Waynesville in the foreground. Knight's Store, built by D. T. Knight in 1901, operated until 1979, when his grandson, Bill Knight, was no longer able to run it, according to Carol Lynn Knight of Balsam, who is married to Bill Knight's son, Balfour Knight. The first Knight's Store was at Willets, but D. T. Knight moved to Balsam when the railroad depot opened there. The house on the right is abandoned now but was once the home of W. B. and Betsy Farwell. (Courtesy of the *Sylva Herald*.)

The exact date of the downtown photograph (below) is not known, but it has to be between 1906, when the Hooper House (front right) was constructed, and 1914, when the courthouse was completed. The Hooper House, which is now home to the Jackson County Chamber of Commerce and Travel and Tourism Authority, is the only structure visible that is still standing. The Sylva First United Methodist Church (back right) is still in the same location, though the church facilities have expanded over the years. Other prominent buildings, generally from left to right, include the Osborne Buchanan home (front left) at the west end of Main Street opposite the Hooper House; the Dillard and Mollie Love house that was an Episcopal church and school; the Judson Allen (later W. W. Watt) home; the Billy Davis house, later known as the Pangle house; and the Henry Curtis house. (Courtesy of Bill Shuler.)

Sylva's famous courthouse was only one year old in 1915 when Jackson County's remaining Civil War veterans gathered on its steps for the dedication of a monument in their honor. That ceremony took place 50 years after the Civil War ended. (Courtesy of WCU Special Collections.)

Jackson County's most photographed building—its historic courthouse—had rows of evergreens beside its famous steps in the above photograph, which was taken around 1950. Two-way traffic, which ended in 1956, was still in effect, as evidenced by the road signs signaling motorists to bear right at the west end of Main Street. N.C. 107 no longer goes through downtown as it once did; instead, the Sylva–to–South Carolina highway now begins at Kel-Save. The courthouse was constructed in 1913 after a special election that moved the county seat from Webster to the then-booming railroad town of Sylva. The original red bricks, still visible in the above photograph, were painted white in the late 1960s. (Courtesy of the *Sylva Herald*.)

The famed Jackson County Courthouse appeared topless in this November 1994 photograph, taken just after the cupola was removed for repairs, which were completed in the historic structure's parking lot. Once the dome's restoration was complete, it was painted white, replacing the former green color, and replaced in May 1995. A complete paint job during the summer of 1997 dressed the 93-year-old courthouse in ice cream colors of lemony cream and lime. More renovations and paint in 2004–2005 restored the structure's familiar white walls and dark green dome. Commissioners decided in 2007 to incorporate the courthouse into a new county library. (Courtesy of the *Sylva Herald*.)